*By the grace of G-d*

# JUDAISM
## IN A
# NUTSHELL

Dovid Zaklikowski

HASIDIC
archives

In conjunction with The Aleph Institute

ISBN 978-1-944875-12-1

Design and Layout by Chaya M. Kanner

Printed in China

*For my grandfather*
*Rabbi Chaim Meir Bukiet*

# TABLE OF CONTENTS

## DIVINE SERVICE

## BETWEEN US

# THE
# FOUNDATION

# G-D

*The infinite Creator of the universe cannot be described by finite human beings. Biblical metaphors abound, but G-d has no gender, no "strong hand" or "outstretched arm." These are meager tools to speak about something unutterable. Indeed, we do not pronounce the name of G-d, and many refrain from writing it, even in translation (hence the hyphen). With this in mind, here is what Judaism tells us about G-d:*

*G-d is One.* Perhaps the best description of G-d is the *Shema* prayer (see below), recited several times each day by observant Jews. "G-d is our L-rd, G-d is One" (Deuteronomy 6:4) is more than simply a declaration of monotheism; "G-d is One," the sages explain, means that all of creation is one with Him: G-d is everywhere and everything.

*G-d is kind.* The Bible uses thirteen different terms to describe His mercy: "G-d, the merciful and kind; G-d, slow to anger, with tremendous love and truth," begins the verse (Exodus 34:6). Like everything about G-d, however, His kindness, for the most part, is incomprehensible to us. Some compare our efforts to understand it to those of a small child who struggles against the limits her parents set for her own safety. But, faced with the manifold tragedies of human existence, we refrain from offering any kind of explanation.

*G-d is caring.* Divine providence is the idea that G-d is intimately involved with His creations on a moment-by-moment basis. The Hasidic masters explain that not a leaf falls from a tree without G-d's "hand" behind it. It follows that there is a divine purpose in everything we experience, and it is our responsibility to make those experiences meaningful and to learn from them.

*G-d wants us to know Him.* What could an infinite, omnipotent being need from finite creations? Nothing. Nevertheless, the Kabbalists explain that G-d gives us a way to connect with Him. The Torah (see the following page) and the commandments (see *Mitzvah*) are gifts, allowing us to grasp something of G-d's wisdom and fulfill the infinite will, thus forming the most improbable and inexplicable relationship that ever existed: the partnership between G-d and human beings.

# TORAH

The word Torah refers to the Five Books of Moses (the Pentateuch), though it is also used loosely for all Jewish teachings.

In 1313 BCE, G-d gave the Torah to the Jewish nation on Mount Sinai (see *Shavuot*). The first two books, Genesis and Exodus, describe the Creation of the world, the lives of the patriarchs and matriarchs, the Israelites' Exodus from Egypt, and the first half-year of their sojourn in the desert. They also contain some of the Torah's 613 commandments (see *Mitzvah*), which comprise all of Jewish observance. The last three books, Leviticus, Numbers, and Deuteronomy, enumerate the rest of the commandments and provide the rest of the Israelites' travels in the desert. The five books, together with the scriptures—Prophets ("*Neviim*") and Writings ("*Ketuvim*")—are called the Tanach, the complete Hebrew Bible.

Complementing and explaining the written Bible are the Mishnah and the Talmud. They are also called the "Oral Law," because G-d communicated them orally to Moses at Sinai, and they are an indispensable part of the Torah. (The Mishnah was finally written down in the second century CE.) Kabbalah, the mystical dimension of the Torah, was for generations reserved for only the most accomplished scholars. However, in the nineteenth century, the Hasidic movement popularized its study, and today it is an indispensable aid to understanding the deeper significance of Creation and observance.

Every generation has its Torah scholars, and their teachings and interpretations are incorporated into the body of rabbinic literature. Not without reason are Jews known as the people of the book. Torah is G-d's wisdom, expressed in human terms, and studying it allows our finite intellect to grasp the infinite. It is the guidebook for life, from cradle to death. The word *Torah* comes from the Hebrew root meaning "lesson." Indeed, profound lessons may be learned from every part of the Torah, even those that seem superfluous or simply entertaining.

In Jewish communities today, Torah is studied by children and adults, laypeople and scholars. There are those who dedicate their entire lives to its study.

# MITZVAH

Though often used loosely to mean any good deed, mitzvah literally means "commandment."

The Torah contains 613 mitzvahs, which are expressions of divine will. While observing commandments may seem like an infringement of personal freedom, in reality, they are G-d's "user's manual" for a rich and fulfilling life.

Judaism views the mitzvahs as opportunities to elevate oneself to a higher spiritual level. Indeed, the word *mitzvah* shares a root with the word "connection," and the commandments are often likened to a rope with 613 individual strands, binding the Jew to G-d.

Mitzvahs are divided into 365 positive commandments (e.g., "respect your elders") and 248 negative ones (e.g., "do not murder"). The sages enacted seven additional mitzvahs, making for a total of 620 general precepts, which themselves have been broken down into detailed observances.

The commandments may also be divided between those that govern a person's relationship with others, like those mentioned above, and those strictly between the person and G-d, such as observing the Sabbath or keeping kosher. (Note that today, in the absence of the Holy Temple in Jerusalem, many Jewish observances cannot be observed until the rebuilding of the Third Temple [see *The*

*Messiah*].)

The Kabbalists offer a deeper insight into the purpose of mitzvahs: G-d created this world because He desired "a dwelling place below," they write. The physical world appears to have little connection with spirituality, yet G-d desires that His presence be revealed, even here. This merging of spiritual and physical is achieved through mitzvahs—physical acts performed for a divine purpose.

Most mitzvahs can be done anywhere (no synagogue needed), by anyone, regardless of their level of observance or knowledge. The sages add that every person, even a sinful one, is filled with mitzvahs as a pomegranate is filled with seeds. Each good deed creates an eternal bond with G-d that can never be severed, no matter what a person chooses to do afterward.

# FREE CHOICE

Human beings are created with two inclinations, one generous and altruistic: G-dly, the other selfish and hedonistic: animalistic. G-d grants us free will so that we may choose between right and wrong, and this freedom is what separates humans from animals.

Free choice makes observance meaningful. Without the so-called "negative inclination," there would be no merit in doing good. The effort required to overcome our negative instincts raises us to a higher spiritual level and elevates the physical world around us, creating, in the language of the Kabbalists, a "dwelling place for G-d."

The apparent conflict between G-d's foreknowledge and our free choice has several resolutions. Some compare it to a spouse who "knows" how their partner will react in a given situation, but does not control their ability to choose an unexpected course. In truth, however, like all of G-d's attributes, G-d's knowledge is beyond our understanding and transcends the limits of the metaphor used to describe it.

Though some ethical traditions have focused on eradicating the evil inclination, Hasidic thought views it as a force with the potential to elevate the individual to greater heights. Strong physical desires may be channeled into pure, spiritual pursuits, thus uplifting and harnessing them in the service of G-d. "Love G-d, your L-rd, with all your heart, with all your soul, and with all your might," the verse says (Deuteronomy 6:5), and our sages interpret *with all your heart* to be: with both the animalistic and the G-dly souls.

# PURPOSE

Human beings are an unlikely combination of spiritual and physical, body and soul. Before "descending" into a body, the soul exists in a world of spiritual delight. Yet G-d desires that the soul be invested in a body and endure the hardships of physical existence because only in the struggle to do good (see *Free Choice*) can it fulfill its true purpose. That is, to reveal G-d's presence in the physical world. Through this struggle, say the mystics, the soul itself reaches greater heights, like a seed that must be placed under the earth before it can sprout into a tall, fruitful tree.

In addition to this general mission, every person has a specific, individual purpose, tailored to their abilities and talents. This mission is often fraught with challenges and difficulties, but it is our responsibility to use our gifts to the fullest and omit no opportunity to do a good deed. For who knows? It may be that for this very purpose we were created.

# JOY

Joy is an essential ingredient in Jewish observance. The biblical narrative recounts that the Israelites were punished because they did not serve G-d "with happiness and a glad heart" (Deuteronomy 28:47). Yet, especially in modern times, there is confusion about what joy is and how to achieve it. Joy is not happiness, for one may feel joy in miserable conditions. Neither is it pleasure, or the unrestrained exuberance for which it is often mistaken.

Joy is a heightened state of mind achieved through meditation and personal effort. A joyous person may be in terrible pain, or they may be dancing and singing. What defines them is not the expression on their face, but their inner sense of *purpose*, even in the face of adversity.

Some have compared the requirements of Jewish observance to a heavy load. If a person realizes that the sack they carry is full of diamonds, they will shoulder the weight with joy—the heavier the better. The Hasidic masters encourage us to develop this perspective about all of life's challenges. Since everything is divine providence, it follows that even our most difficult days are part of G-d's master plan, a means for us to fulfill our purpose in life. This thought, when internalized, brings an energy and peace of mind that makes tackling the challenges much easier.

"Worship G-d with joy," says the Psalmist (100:2), and the Kabbalists add: this is the key to serving G-d effectively. Conversely, unhappiness, apathy, and self-pity weaken us and make us vulnerable to the enticements of the evil inclination.

# REPENTANCE

The Hebrew word for repentance, *teshuvah*, actually means "return."
This simple word captures Judaism's approach to the subject. If one
strays from the correct path, all that is necessary is to return to one's
true self, which is inherently good and not defined by imperfect actions.
As the verse says, "You will then return to G-d, your L-rd ... with all your
heart and with all your soul" (Deuteronomy 30:2).

The process of *return* is: (1) stop doing the negative actions and, if possible, repair any harm that was done (e.g., return the stolen object); (2) regret the wrong action, and commit to never do it again; and (3) ask forgiveness of those negatively affected by the wrong actions (including G-d). These three steps cleanse the soul from the impurity of wrongdoing.

Judaism celebrates repentance as an unparalleled opportunity for closeness to G-d. The sages say that nothing obstructs the path of those who return to G-d and that even a perfectly righteous person is on a lower level than the returnee. For this reason, the Hasidic teachers explain that *teshuvah* should be done with joy.

A constant focus on wrongdoing and repentance will lead to unhappiness, and thus there are set times for repentance: daily, at the end of morning prayers and before going to bed; on the eve of the new Hebrew month; and during the High Holidays.

# REWARD AND PUNISHMENT

Judaism tells us that there will be reward for those who follow G-d's path and punishment for those who don't. For the most part, these consequences are meted out in the afterlife (see the following page). When a person is rewarded or punished here, it is not immediately discernable, to protect our free choice. Receiving immediate reward makes it difficult to choose wrongly.

That does not mean that observance brings no benefits in this world. On the contrary, a life of Jewish observance is deeply rewarding, both physically and spiritually, and many people experience manifest blessings in their lives that appear to be the result of observance. Still, in these times, it is not possible to draw a direct line between a mitzvah and its reward.

The question of why bad things happen to good people becomes less urgent when we view life as an opportunity to fulfill a mission, often fraught with multiple challenges, rather than a cycle of reward and punishment (see more in *Joy*, *Free Choice*, and *Purpose*). The sages remind us that the greatest reward for observance is the joy of serving our Creator. "The reward for a mitzvah is the mitzvah itself," bringing connection and closeness to the infinite Source of all good.

# AFTERLIFE

Life does not begin at birth and end with death, as the verse states (Ecclesiastes 12:7), "When the dust returns to the ground as it was and the spirit returns to G-d, who bestowed it." Judaism affirms the existence of an eternal soul in every human being. We do not glorify the afterlife at the expense of this world; however, as the sages famously proclaimed, one moment of Torah study and good deeds in this world is worth more than all the spiritual pleasures of the World to Come.

When the body dies, the soul returns to the spiritual world, where it reaps the benefits of the good deeds it performed. But the spiritual world is static. Growth and achievement are only possible in this world.

Judaism's conception of punishment in the afterlife is likewise unique. There is no punishment for the sake of punishment. Rather, the person's wrongdoings are shown to the soul, which now experiences the full magnitude of the spiritual pain it caused. In addition, there are several painful processes that a soul may go through for cleansing purposes so that it can enjoy the spiritual pleasures of the afterlife. The living may ease the pain of this process by performing good deeds and studying Torah on the soul's behalf.

The soul feels its loved ones' pain, rejoices in their joy, and receives satisfaction from their good deeds. For this reason, Jewish law stipulates that a person should not mourn for the deceased more than the allotted time, lest they inadvertently cause their loved one pain.

# THE MESSIAH

Belief in a Messiah, who will redeem and perfect the world, is one of the thirteen core principles of Jewish faith. Known in Hebrew as the *Moshiach* ("anointed one"), he will be a human king who will bring peace to the world and eradicate poverty, hunger, and illness.

The sages enumerate four tasks that the Messiah will perform: (1) bring the entire Jewish nation to observance, (2) battle the enemies of the Jewish nation, (3) build the Holy Temple in Jerusalem, and (4) gather all Jews to the Land of Israel. No one has yet fulfilled these conditions.

Though subjects like the resurrection of the dead have generated intense discussion, we do not know precise details about what life will be like during the Messianic era. As the Jews have said for centuries, when the Messiah comes, we will see.

Belief in the Messiah has sustained the Jewish nation through centuries of persecution and suffering. Countless martyrs have gone to their deaths with the words of the popular song, "I believe, with complete faith, in the coming of the Messiah," on their lips. Their longing for that time was shared by the Kabbalists, who declared it the ultimate purpose of Creation.

Good deeds, especially those that aid other people, bring the Messianic era closer. The sages explain that each mitzvah, each personal triumph over the evil inclination, has the potential to "tip the scale" and transform the entire world for the better.

# DIVINE
# SERVICE

# PRAYER

The Hebrew word for prayer, *tefillah*, comes from the root "to connect." The three daily prayer services are times reserved for introspection and self-refinement in the service of G-d. They are also an opportunity to ask G-d for assistance, and often, the two goals are intertwined.

One may, at any time, turn to G-d in prayer for their personal needs, as the verse states (Deuteronomy 11:13), "Serve Him with all your heart and soul," which refers to prayer, the "service of the heart." Once the Jews were exiled from Jerusalem in 423 BCE, however, the sages instituted three daily prayers in place of the two daily offerings, with the evening prayer representing the burning of the leftover animal parts. Additional prayers were added to correspond to the extra offerings on Sabbath and holidays.

Morning prayers, the primary service of the day, are compared to a ladder, drawing the worshipper upwards. They begin with praises of G-d and creation intended to evoke gratitude and wonder, then proceed to the *Shema* prayer, proclaiming G-d's unity and encompassing presence. During the climax of the service, nineteen blessings recited in a whisper, the worshippers finally ask G-d for their needs. In addition to the three formal services, observant Jews recite blessings throughout the day thanking G-d for almost every aspect of human existence.

Psalms appear frequently in the Jewish liturgy, and many have the custom of reciting additional chapters after services and in times of need. Some complete the entire book monthly, or even weekly, according to a daily schedule.

A good way to prepare for prayer is to study works that explain G-d's greatness, particularly the teachings of Hasidism, which are intended to evoke the feelings of love and awe necessary for prayer. This ensures that it *remains* a service of the heart and does not devolve into rote recitation.

# SHEMA

*The first verse of the prayer known as the Shema (Listen) is the quintessential declaration of monotheism, affirming the Jews' belief in a single, all-encompassing deity.*

The verse (Deuteronomy 6:4), "Listen, O Israel, G-d is our L-rd, G-d is One," with additional verses from Deuteronomy (6:5–9 and 11:13–21) and Numbers (15:37–41), is recited as part of the morning and evening services in fulfillment of the commandment to "speak of them when you are at home, when traveling on the road, when you lie down, and when you get up" (Deuteronomy 6:7).

The sages single out the verse, "Love G-d, your L-rd, with all your heart, with all your soul, and with all your might" (Deuteronomy 6:5) as essential to understanding the *Shema's* meaning. They explain that with "all your heart" means with both the positive and negative inclinations (see *Free Choice*); "with all your soul" indicates the willingness to give up one's life if necessary; and "with all your might" means with all your money.

Jewish law stipulates that it is especially important to meditate on the meaning of the words while saying the *Shema* prayer. Thus, it is customary to avoid distractions by covering one's eyes with the right hand during the first verse. The prayer is also recited before going to sleep and, when possible, around the time when one feels that they are going to pass on (see *Death and Mourning*).

The two names of G-d used in the *Shema* are individually significant. The first, the four-letter, ineffable name of G-d (read as *Ado-nai*, "my Master"), represents G-d's encompassing presence that transcends creation and the comprehension of finite beings. The second, *Elo-heinu* (our G-d), represents the aspect of G-d that is intimately involved in the world. The *Shema*, then, tells us that these two seemingly incompatible qualities are part of one unknowable G-d.

# BLESSINGS

*Blessed are You, L-rd our G-d, King of the universe....* Thus begins every one of the many blessings in Jewish liturgy, recited before eating and drinking, over pleasant smells, when observing natural wonders, in thanks for the various functions of the human body, and before performing most Jewish observances. Including those contained in the prayer services, it is the aim to recite at least one hundred blessings each day.

The sages say that one who enjoys any aspect of creation without reciting a blessing is like one who pockets something belonging to G-d. As King David writes, "The earth and all it contains is G-d's" (Psalms 24:1).

While each mitzvah merits its own individual blessing, food and beverages are divided into general categories: foods that grow on trees; those that grow from the ground; foods made with the grains of wheat, barley, spelt, oats, and rye; and all other foods, which fall under the general blessing, "… who creates everything through His word."

Blessings are intended to foster an attitude of gratitude in the Jew, who sees even the ability to relieve oneself as something to be thankful for. Most significant in Jewish law are the blessings recited after eating, for they fulfill the biblical commandment (Deuteronomy 8:10): "When you eat and are satisfied, you shall bless G-d, your L-rd, for the good land that He has given you."

# KOSHER

*Kosher* literally means "fit," and, though used broadly to mean anything good or appropriate, it usually refers to food that conforms to the requirements of Jewish law.

Leviticus defines a kosher animal as one that both chews its cud and has split hooves (e.g. no pork); kosher fish must have fins and scales (e.g. no shellfish), while insects and many birds (e.g. birds of prey) are prohibited. It is also prohibited to mix meat and milk, a law that the sages extended to include poultry.

The verses make it clear that these restrictions are intended to make us holy. "I am G-d, and I brought you out of Egypt to be your G-d," proclaims Leviticus (11:45). "Therefore, since I am holy, you shall remain holy."

To codify and protect these commandments, the sages instituted detailed kosher laws, which fill volumes. Kosher animals are slaughtered in a specific way by a trained ritual slaughterer, and the meat prepared according to specific guidelines.

One of the most well-known of the kosher laws is the prohibition on mixing meat and milk, as the verse states (Exodus 23:19), "You shall not cook a kid in the milk of its mother." One may not partake of dairy products for several hours after eating meat, and one may not cook or eat dairy with utensils or dishes used for meat.

The food we eat becomes part of us, and it seems wise to follow the dietary guidelines that G-d, who is called the Healer of All Flesh, gave. The sages add that consuming non-kosher food not only affects the body, but also makes us less sensitive to the soul.

The complex kosher laws make it necessary for processed foods to be produced under the supervision of an expert trained in kosher dietary laws. Kosher symbols, which indicate the name of the supervising agency, can be found on many products around the world.

# MEZUZAH

*A mezuzah is a small roll of parchment inscribed with biblical verses, specifically, the* Shema *prayer. The word literally means "doorpost," because the scrolls are affixed on the upper portion of the right-hand doorpost (as one enters the room) in a Jewish home or business in fulfillment of the commandment to "write them [these words] on the doorposts of your houses and on your gates" (Deuteronomy 6:9).*

As the verse implies, the purpose of a mezuzah is to remind the building's occupants of G-d's presence. Thus, many have a custom to touch or kiss the mezuzah as they leave or enter a building or room. The scrolls, usually encased in small boxes, also serve to uplift and sanctify the structure itself.

On the back of each mezuzah scroll, the scribe writes the name of G-d associated with protection, leading the sages to observe that kings of flesh and blood are surrounded with guards who are exposed to danger, while the King of kings Himself guards the homes of His people.

# TEFILLIN

Tefillin are black leather boxes containing parchment scrolls inscribed with biblical verses. The two boxes, secured with leather straps on the arm and head, are worn by men over the age of thirteen during morning prayers (excluding the Sabbath and major Jewish holidays) to fulfill the commandment, "These words which I am commanding you ... bind them as a sign on your hand, and let them be an emblem in the center of your head" (Deuteronomy 6:6, 8).

Some of the verses inside the tefillin pertain to the Exodus from Egypt, and wearing tefillin is also a way to fulfill one's obligation to remember the Exodus daily. Though it is best to wear the tefillin during prayers, the mitzvah can be performed by simply donning them for a brief time and reciting the *Shema* prayer anytime during the day until sunset (see *Calendar*). On the Sabbath and major holidays, one does not don tefillin.

The arm tefillin are worn on the bicep of the non-dominant arm, facing the heart, and the straps are wound three times around the bicep, seven times on the forearm, once on the hand, and three times on the middle finger, signifying the worshipper's binding himself in G-d's service. The head tefillin are placed just above the forehead, centered between the eyes, with the back knot lying on base of the skull. The boxes' proximity to the heart and brain are intended to uplift those organs and remind the Jew to dedicate both his intellect and emotions to G-d.

# KIPPAH

Called a yarmulke *in Yiddish, a kippah is a skullcap worn by Jewish men and boys, symbolizing their awareness of G-d above.*

Though there is no commandment to wear a kippah, the practice has become an important part of Jewish observance. Even those who do not wear a kippah at all times make a point of covering their heads when praying, studying Torah, reciting a blessing, or entering a synagogue.

Many communities use distinctive kippahs of various sizes, colors, and designs. Some are intricate works of art, such as those made by Jewish artisans from Yemen and Georgia.

# IMMERSION

*Immersion, as an act of spiritual purification, plays an important role in Jewish life. People and utensils may be purified by being immersed in a body of "living water." Though an ocean or spring-fed lake, under specific circumstances, will suffice, most immersion today is performed in* mikvahs, *ritual baths built to the specifications of Jewish law.*

A new convert to Judaism immerses as the final step in the lengthy conversion process; a body is immersed as a final rite of purification before burial (see *Death and Mourning*); and most new pots, dishes, and utensils are dunked before they can be used.

The most widespread users of mikvahs, however, are women. A week after the woman's monthly cycle, as a prelude to resuming a physical relationship with her husband, she immerses in a mikvah. This practice has nothing to do with physical impurity. Rather, it is a spiritual renewal, an acknowledgement of the possibility for life that has been lost and the new opportunity that is beginning.

Men traditionally immerse in a mikvah before holidays and important occasions, such as their wedding day. Some have a custom to immerse weekly before the Sabbath, or even daily before prayers.

One of the many explanations offered for this mitzvah: Immersion is a rebirth. Just as a fetus in the womb is submerged in water and emerges into the world pure, one who enters a mikvah erases past impurities and begins anew.

# STUDY

Perhaps more than any other observance, Torah study characterizes the Jewish way of life. The obligation to study Torah, defined broadly here as the entire body of Jewish teachings, begins in early childhood and continues until one's passing. In study halls around the world, one finds young students, the elderly, and professionals, dropping in for a few minutes after work, sitting together, all equally immersed in the study of G-d's teachings.

The source of the mitzvah to study Torah is found in Deuteronomy: "Listen, Israel, to the rules and laws that I am publicly declaring to you today. Learn from them and safeguard them, so that you will be able to keep them" (5:1). The sages note that although Jewish observance is more important than Torah study, Torah study is ultimately greater, because it leads to deed. Continuous study not only vitalizes one's performance of the observance—the Hasidic masters explain that by studying Torah, a Jew can achieve an extraordinary union with G-d, as the finite intellect engages with and grasps infinite wisdom.

Torah books are treated with the utmost respect in a Jewish home. If a volume falls on the floor, it is customary to immediately pick it up and give it a kiss, an expression of reverence and love for the G-dly wisdom it contains.

Parents are required to teach their children Torah ("Teach them to your children" [ibid.]), an obligation that can be fulfilled through a surrogate if they are unable to fulfill it themselves.

# SAFETY AND STEWARDSHIP

While everything that happens is divine providence, we are not allowed to tempt fate. A bad ladder should not be kept in a house where it may come to be used. Neither should a dangerous animal be kept as a pet. In the words of the verse, "Place a fence around your roof. Do not allow a dangerous situation to remain in your house" (Deuteronomy 22:8). A person may be destined to be hurt by falling off a roof, but it is our responsibility to ensure that we are not the conduits for this unfortunate decree.

Similarly, we are required to care for and conserve natural resources: "You shall not destroy its trees, wielding an ax against any food-producing tree" (Deuteronomy 20:19). Nothing that can be used by a human being should be thrown out or destroyed—the sages go so far as to say that one may not cause a candle to burn more quickly than it otherwise would.

This law does not apply in situations where destroying one thing will benefit others. People are permitted to slaughter animals for meat; a tree that is preventing the growth of others or an animal that is a menace may be destroyed; and if there is no other wood that can be used, one is permitted to destroy furniture to heat a house.

These laws embody the Torah's value for sensitivity and compassion. As the sages say, one who begins destroying inanimate objects will ultimately come to destroy others, and himself.

# BETWEEN US

# FELLOWSHIP

"Love your fellow as you love yourself" (Leviticus 19:18) was singled out by the sages of the Talmud as the foundation on which all observance rests. As one sage said, "That which you do not like, do not do to another. This is the entire Torah; the rest is commentary."

Deceptively simple, difficult to achieve, on the most basic level it means that we should overlook the faults of others, just as we overlook our own. Some point out that the verse in Leviticus (ibid.) ends with "I am G-d," since only G-d can know our intentions, while no man may truly know what lies in the other's heart. Refraining from judgment is the first step.

The commandment also requires us to assist those who need help, be it physical or spiritual. This task is made easier when we approach them with love and understanding.

The Hasidic masters add that the souls of all Israel in fact comprise one large body, with each individual limb performing a different function. One should not despise one's neighbor just like the brain does not despise the heart—each is necessary for the proper functioning of the whole.

# CHARITY

"The poor will never cease to exist in the land, so I am commanding you to open your hand generously to your poor and destitute in your land" (Deuteronomy 15:11). Charity, known in Hebrew as *tzedakah* (righteousness), is an ethical obligation for every Jew, no matter their financial status. By giving charity, the individual acknowledges that they are part of a larger community. It is their obligation to aid the other members of the community, thus creating a more just, more perfect world.

There is no minimum required amount—though tithing, giving at least one-tenth of one's income, is desirable (one should not give charity at the expense of their family's needs). Of course, the most effective form of charity is to provide someone with a livelihood. Free loan societies (due to the prohibition of charging interest) can be found in most Jewish communities.

Anonymous charity is considered the highest form, allowing the recipients to maintain their dignity. Even better, "double-blind" giving, in which the giver does not know who has received the money, protects donors from undue feelings of pride. The Jewish aid organizations found in every community offer just this kind of giving opportunity.

The act of giving benefits the giver as well as the receiver, ingraining traits like generosity and kindness, and many make a habit of giving numerous times each day. Charity boxes are a fixture in many homes (literally, many even nail them to the wall), and a common custom is to place some coins in one before beginning to pray. Despite its importance, no blessing is recited over this observance to ensure that one in need of help receives it without delay.

# BUSINESS

Man was created to toil: "Six days of the week you shall work" (Exodus 20:8). *How* we make our living is our own affair, as long as it is ethical and honest.

Unethical business practices have their root in envy. The sages point to the tenth commandment, not to covet that which is your neighbor's, as the source of all cheating. If one truly believes and accepts that G-d will give them what they need, there would be no incentive to do wrong. "Who is wealthy?" they famously asked. "One who is happy with his lot."

Taking advantage of a customer's ignorance by charging more than the going rate for a product or service, selling an item with a hidden defect, or using an inaccurate scale (merchants are required to calibrate their scales regularly to avoid this transgression) are all prohibited. Negative advertising is also frowned upon, especially when it will detract from the livelihood of another.

This may all seem like common sense, but, as many experienced businesspeople will tell you, dishonesty in business is a slippery slope. A tiny deception can lead to a much bigger one, and Judaism emphasizes that scrupulous honesty in business is an expression of respect and love, not just for one's fellow, but for G-d.

# KINDNESS

The general imperative to "love your fellow" is broken down into several more specific observances: visiting the sick, welcoming guests, bringing joy to a bride and groom, caring for the deceased, and comforting a mourner.

Several of these are derived from a well-known episode in the book of Genesis. Abraham, the first Jew, had circumcised himself three days earlier and was recovering outside his tent when G-d appeared to him (performing, the commentaries point out, the mitzvah of visiting the sick). A few moments later, three strangers approach Abraham's tent, and he interrupts his tête-à-tête with G-d to run and greet them, thus showing that welcoming guests trumps even a divine revelation (18:1–2).

The sages emphasize that these deeds cannot be performed in a perfunctory manner. Guests should be escorted to the front door as they leave; sick people and mourners are treated with extra consideration so that they do not feel worse after the visit than they did before.

Like honesty in business, these things may not seem to require a divine imperative. But real, selfless kindness is not easy to achieve. Making it part of our divine service encourages us to strive for it. We may never get there, but we will do a lot of good along the way.

# SPEECH

Gossip, often treated as a harmless pastime, is a serious transgression. The prohibition of "evil speech" includes repeating negative things about someone, even when they are true. "You shall not go around as a gossipmonger amidst your people" (Leviticus 19:16). Of course, the most harmful form of gossip is slander.

Judaism takes gossip seriously because it recognizes the power of speech: speaking well of someone can encourage them to do better; carefully chosen words can bring peace between a husband and wife. By the same token, however, speaking badly of someone, even if they do not hear it, will strengthen their negative qualities, as well as those of the person who is listening.

For this reason, when not needed for a precise ruling, the Torah uses positive words and avoids negative ones. For instance, rather than use the negative word *impure*, G-d instructs Noah to take "the clean beasts and of the beasts that *are not* clean" into the Ark (Genesis 7:8). The Torah also praises Noah as a "righteous man" to build him up during difficult times.

Note that the transgression of gossip applies equally to the speaker and the listener. Juicy rumors should be avoided at all costs, even if it means walking away from the conversation.

# RESPECT

Respect for elders, for Torah scholars, and for parents is an integral part of Jewish life. "Stand up before [one who has] a white head," the Torah commands, "and give respect to the old" (Leviticus 19:32). Age brings wisdom that cannot be acquired any other way. The sages point out that the verse ends with, "you shall thus fear G-d" to indicate that respecting elders is akin to respecting G-d.

Torah scholars, as receptacles of divine wisdom, are given great respect—one is required to stand when they enter a room.

One should also respect their parents, as the verse states (Exodus 20:11), "Honor your father and mother." In fact, it is fifth of the Ten Commandments, falling under the category of commandments "between man and G-d" (see *Mitzvah*), because one's parents partnered with G-d to bring a child into the world.

# THE
# LIFE CYCLE

# BIRTH

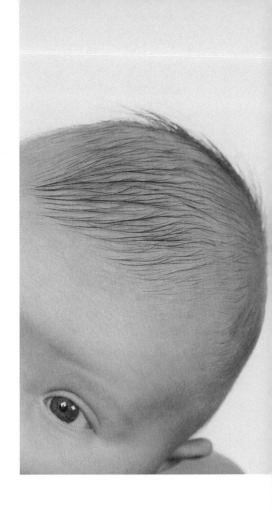

Procreation is a privilege
and an obligation in
Jewish life. The first
commandment to the
first two humans, "Be
fruitful and multiply and
fill the earth" (Genesis
1:28), is an opportunity
to partner with G-d in
the act of creation.

Healthy baby boys are circumcised on the eighth day after birth. The *brit* (literally "covenant") is performed by a professional circumciser (*mohel*), who has extensive training in this area. Because the health of the child is paramount, if there is any question about whether he is strong enough, the circumcision is postponed.

According to Jewish tradition, Elijah the Prophet attends every circumcision, making it an especially holy occasion. It is considered a great honor to hold the baby during the ceremony, and the baby is given his Jewish name at this time as well. Participants join in a festive meal afterwards.

Circumcision has been banned in various countries throughout history and continues to be the subject of controversy to this day. Nevertheless, it has been preserved, with considerable sacrifice, and is one of the few mitzvahs routinely performed by even the most assimilated Jews. The sages explain that removing the foreskin symbolizes the sanctification and dedication of the body—with all its physical drives and passions—to G-d.

Girls are named with a special prayer recited during the Torah reading in the synagogue, and celebrated with a festive meal after Sabbath services, usually held in the synagogue. Using a Hebrew name in daily life is a sign of pride in one's heritage and identity.

# BAR AND BAT MITZVAH

## COMING OF AGE

Children are encouraged to perform mitzvahs as soon as they are able to for educational purposes. They are not obligated to do so, however, until they are a bar or bat mitzvah (son or daughter of the mitzvah)— which occurs on the girl's twelfth, and boy's thirteenth Jewish birthday. On that day, they assume the status of a Jewish adult—subject to all the obligations of Jewish observance—and this monumental event should be the focus of the day.

On a basic level, the bar and bat mitzvah should be celebrated like any other birthday—a day for extra Torah study, reciting Psalms, giving charity, and celebration. Some have the custom to eat a fruit that has just come into season, so as to be able to recite the blessing reserved for special occasions. On this occasion, all this is done more publicly and with added flair, at a gathering of family and friends, and the boy or girl delivers a speech about the significance of the day, including words of Torah.

A boy begins to put on tefillin just prior to bar mitzvah so that he has time to practice. On the Shabbat closest to his birthday (some choose a Monday or Thursday), he is called up to make a blessing on the Torah during the reading of the weekly portion. Often, he reads the portion himself.

Public service projects have become a popular element of the bar and bat mitzvah experience, and, though praiseworthy, they are not a requirement. The lavish after-parties that are the norm in many communities are likewise unnecessary, and often represent a gratuitous expense for parents.

Jewish custom is that on joyous days (e.g., holidays and weddings), the prayers requesting G-d's forgiveness for sins are not recited. The exemption does not apply to a bar or bat mitzvah, however, because repentance is an integral part of Jewish life. On the day of their initiation, the young person has the comfort of knowing that there is always a path to return (see *Repentance*).

# MARRIAGE

Genesis concludes the account of Adam's marriage to Eve with the words, "Therefore a man shall leave his father and his mother and cleave to his wife, and they shall become one flesh" (2:24). Uniting a man and woman, the sages tell us, is as difficult as splitting the sea.

Jewish weddings are performed under a canopy (*chupah*), and begin with the bride walking around the groom seven times, representing the encompassing presence of G-d and the "new domain" that the couple is entering together. The actual term for marriage is derived from the word *holy* or *separate*—the couple has chosen each other and pledged their devotion to the exclusion of all others, and this is the content of the first blessing, recited before the ring is placed by the groom on the bride's finger. The marriage contract (*ketubah*) is read; six more blessings are recited over a cup of wine, of which both bride and groom partake afterwards; and, perhaps most famously, the groom breaks a glass under his foot in remembrance of the Holy Temple, because the pain of its destruction cannot be forgotten, even at such a happy time. The wedding concludes with a feast and joyous dancing.

As befits such a holy occasion, the bride and groom spend the first part of their wedding day fasting, praying, and giving charity, laying a spiritual foundation upon which they will draw in the years to come. The sages tell us that marriage is the reunion of a single soul that has been placed in two separate bodies, and thus a good cause for celebration.

# DEATH AND MOURNING

Judaism celebrates life. Death is cause for mourning, as the body is no longer able to participate in the perfection of creation. In Judaism, one does not attempt to preserve, make a relic of, or cremate the body, "For dust you are, and to dust you will return" (Genesis 3:19). Once the soul has departed, the body is immersed in a body of water or washed in a specific way, dressed in white shrouds, and placed in a simple wooden coffin. These tasks are detailed and complex, and thus are performed by trained laypeople. For the peace of the soul, the funeral is held as soon as possible after the passing. It is considered a good deed to walk with the coffin on its way to the cemetery (*levaya*, the Hebrew term for a funeral, literally means "to accompany"). At the funeral itself, the immediate family members make a symbolic tear in their garments; the special prayer of sanctification (*Kaddish*) is recited; the family places the first layer of dirt over the coffin and afterwards walks between two rows of people who comfort them. Participating in a funeral is called a "true kindness," since the favor cannot be repaid by the deceased.

Immediate family members observe *shiva*, a seven-day period of intense mourning after the funeral, during which they do not bathe, wear new clothing, study Torah, or do business. Mourners spend much of the seven days sitting on low chairs and receiving visitors who come to console them. These formal observances are intended as tools to express their grief.

After the first week, there is an additional twenty-three-day period of less intense mourning, and for the next eleven months, at least one child, parent, or sibling of the deceased recites the *Kaddish* prayer three times a day during prayer services (when a family member cannot recite it, someone may be designated to do it for the family). After that, the prayer is recited on the anniversary of passing (*yahrtzeit*), when many have a custom to give charity or sponsor events on behalf of the deceased. Mourning that goes beyond these customs is considered inappropriate and disrespectful to the loved one, who is now in the "World of Truth" and appreciates the infinite wisdom of Torah.

Though it is closely associated with mourning and death, the *Kaddish* prayer makes no mention of these subjects. Rather, it is a prayer about the holiness and transcendence of G-d. To mourners, it is a message of comfort. G-d, in His infinite wisdom, chose to take the soul of their loved one at the time that it was intended to depart this world. To the congregation, which listens and answers "amen," it is a powerful declaration of faith, spoken by those who have endured great pain.

# THE
# YEAR CYCLE

# CALENDAR

The Hebrew calendar is lunisolar: the months are determined by the cycle of the moon, but since the lunar year is 354 days, an extra month is added every two or three years to keep up with the 365-day solar year. These frequent leap years ensure that holidays are celebrated in their proper seasons—Passover in the spring, Sukkot in the autumn.

In Temple times, the calendar was set by the rabbinic court in Jerusalem, which determined the length of each month based on testimony from witnesses who had seen the new moon. It took time for the communities outside of the Land of Israel to receive the news about when a new month began, so they celebrated each holiday for two days, just in case. This practice continues in the Diaspora until today, though we now use a set calendar based on mathematical calculations.

The days of the Jewish month begin at nightfall based on the verse's account of the first day: "And it was evening and it was morning, one day" (Genesis 1:5). Jewish calendars, which give the Hebrew dates and times for the beginning of each holiday as they correspond to the Gregorian dates, are easy to find, both online and in print. Note that the times for sunrise, sunset, and nightfall will vary by location and time of year.

Why a lunar calendar? The Jewish nation has been compared to the moon. Its fortunes have waxed and waned throughout history. Sometimes it seems to be completely extinguished, yet it always renews itself. In this spirit, once a month, after evening services, there is a prayer to say while standing outside after dark to sanctify and bless the moon while it is visible.

# TIME

Judaism takes time seriously. G-d created time on the first day of Creation: "G-d said, 'Let there be light,' and there was light ... and G-d separated between the light and between the darkness" (Genesis 1:1–3). The three daily prayers are recited by specific times in order to be valid, and some observances may be performed only during certain periods of the day.

These periods are determined by the sun and stars, and vary widely by season and location. For instance, the afternoon prayer is recited a half hour after midday (the halfway point between sunrise and sunset) until sunset. In the days before clocks and watches, observing these requirements took considerable thought and planning. Nowadays, the times for prayer are widely available and easy to observe.

Judaism's reverence for time is not small-minded. Life is precious and limited. Counting the minutes between sunrise and sunset brings home the lesson that each moment is an opportunity to fulfill our mission in this world, an opportunity that will never be available again.

# SABBATH

*The Jewish Sabbath, in Hebrew, Shabbat, is observed from sunset on Friday until after nightfall on Saturday (all Jewish holidays begin in the evening) and is a day of rest and pleasure.*

Shabbat commemorates the completion of the six days of Creation and G-d's resting on the seventh day. Observing Shabbat is one of the Ten Commandments: "Six days you shall labor and do all your work; but the seventh day is a Sabbath unto the L-rd, your G-d" (Exodus 20:9).

Practically, observing Shabbat means refraining from performing creative work, as defined by Jewish law, and sanctifying the day by reciting special prayers and partaking of three festive meals, one on Friday night and two on Saturday.

The holy day is ushered in by the women and girls of the family, who light candles before sunset (in the absence of women, a man should light them). In the past, Shabbat candles were a literal source of light— kindling a flame on the Sabbath is not permitted—and prevented people from stumbling in the dark. Today, they are a spiritual one. The sages say that the Shabbat candles bring peace to the home and beyond, and the moment of kindling them is considered an auspicious time when a woman can ask G-d for whatever she needs. In many communities, girls begin lighting a candle, with the assistance of a parent, as soon as they can recite the blessing. A married woman lights two candles and many have the custom to add one for each child.

The Friday night and Saturday day meals begin with *Kiddush*, a prayer sanctifying the day, traditionally recited over wine, and a blessing over two loaves of bread. The family dresses in their finest clothes and partakes of special delicacies to honor the Sabbath.

Shabbat is often called "an island in time," when weekday labors and cares are put aside, and we can dedicate ourselves to G-d and family. In today's world, it is particularly significant that no technology may be used on Shabbat, allowing families to spend quality time together.

# ROSH HASHANAH

## NEW YEAR

*Rosh Hashanah (literally, "head of the year") is observed on the first and second days of the Hebrew month of Tishrei (usually during September) and begins the High Holiday season. It is a day of judgment, when G-d "inscribes" the fate of each person for the following year. It is also a day of rededication to divine service, a day to crown G-d as our King.*

The three themes of the holiday—coronation, remembrance, and judgment—are personified in the central observance of the day, the sounding of a hollowed-out ram's horn, known as a *shofar*. "And in the seventh month, on the first day, there shall be a holy convocation for you; you shall not perform any mundane work. It shall be a day of sounding the horn" (Numbers 29:1). The shofar is blown multiple times during the longer-than-usual prayer services.

The shofar recalls the binding of Isaac, when Abraham was granted a reprieve from sacrificing his only son and sacrificed a ram in its place. By sounding the shofar on the day of judgment, we invoke the righteousness of our patriarch as a merit. Its unique sound has also been compared to the cry of a child, in this case the soul, who yearns to repent and reconnect to her source. Others liken it to the trumpets blown at the coronation of a human king.

Sweet foods, particularly apples dipped in honey, are part of the traditional Rosh Hashanah table, physical embodiments of the sweet year to come. Some have the custom to eat the head of a fish or other animal so that "we should be heads and not tails." Pomegranates remind us that we should be filled with mitzvahs as a pomegranate is filled with seeds.

On the first afternoon of the holiday, it is customary to walk to a body of water that contains live fish and symbolically cast one's sins into the water to be consumed. The source of this practice is a verse in the book of Micah: "You shall cast into the depths of the sea all their sins" (7:19).

Though the Rosh Hashanah liturgy describes it as the day the world was created, it is actually the anniversary of the creation of man. This means that creation was completed only on the sixth day, with Adam and Eve, and that G-d entrusted this world to humans, who, by crowning G-d as their King, become partners with Him in creation. Rosh Hashanah is a yearly reminder that we are not here to exploit and destroy, but to perfect and sanctify the world and to serve the Creator.

# YOM KIPPUR

## THE DAY OF ATONEMENT

The introspection and repentance of Rosh Hashanah culminate in a day of fasting and prayer on the tenth day of the Jewish month of Tishrei: Yom Kippur is the most sacred day on the Jewish calendar.

"It is a day of atonement. It shall be a holy occasion for you; you shall afflict yourselves" (Leviticus 23:27). On Yom Kippur we abstain from eating and drinking, and do not wash, apply cream, wear leather shoes, or have marital relations. This is also an effort to emulate the angels, who have no physical needs. It is customary to immerse in a mikvah (see *Immersion*) before the holiday begins and to dress in white, a sign of purity: "If your sins prove to be [stained] like [the color] crimson, they will become white as snow" (Isaiah 1:18).

Yom Kippur is a day of atonement for transgressions between man and G-d. The sages make clear, however, that G-d cannot forgive us for wrongs done to other people, so it's advisable to ask forgiveness before the holiday from those we have wronged in order to completely clear our slate.

Yom Kippur is the day when Moses descended from Mount Sinai with the second set of tablets. The first set were destroyed because of the sin of the golden calf. After the Israelites repented and were punished for their sin, Moses's prayers were accepted, he went back up the mountain and received the second set, and G-d told him, "I have forgiven them" (Numbers 14:20).

Despite its rigorous observances, Yom Kippur is a joyful day. The opportunity to regret our past negative actions and return to G-d is a mitzvah to be celebrated and a gift to be treasured. The assurance that our return will be accepted brings great joy.

# SUKKOT

The solemn tone of the first two High Holidays gives way to undisguised joy on Sukkot, "the time of your rejoicing." The holiday is named after the small hut (*sukkah*) which becomes our home for the entire seven days.

A temporary dwelling roofed with leaves or vegetation (e.g., pine branches or bamboo) that are detached from their source, the sukkah commemorates the Israelites' journey through the desert, when they lived in small booths: "For a seven-day period you shall live in booths ... in order that your [ensuing] generations should know that I had the Children

of Israel live in booths when I took them out of the land of Egypt"
(Leviticus 23:42–3).

Jewish law provides specific guidelines for a sukkah: it should have at
least three walls that will withstand the wind and a roof with direct
access to the sky. The most distinctive part of the sukkah is its roof,
which is made of unrefined greenery, dense enough that there is more
shade than sunlight, but spread out enough that the inhabitants can still
see the stars. Commentaries note that Sukkot falls in the autumn, when
the weather is often cold and rainy, to make it clear that this mitzvah is
not for our physical comfort. Indeed, living in the sukkah is intended
to bring home the temporary nature of our existence, our vulnerability,
and our dependence on G-d's blessings.

On a deeper level, dwelling in a sukkah is one of the few mitzvahs that
can be performed with the entire body, rather than just a single limb.
The sages note that the encompassing nature of Sukkot makes it a time
of unity, both with G-d and among the Jewish people themselves.

The second mitzvah of Sukkot is the Four Species. On each day of the
holiday, a palm branch, willow branches, myrtle branches, and a citron

are held together, a blessing is said, and then together they are shaken in four directions, fulfilling the verse, "And you shall take for yourselves on the first day beautiful fruit of trees, branches of the palm tree, date palm fronds, a branch of a braided tree, and willows of the brook, and you shall rejoice before the L-rd, your G-d, for a seven-day period" (ibid. 40).

Among the explanations offered for this observance: The different species represent different types of people. Some have a pleasant smell (representing Jewish observance), others a pleasant taste (Jewish study); some have both, and some have neither, yet all are held together in this commandment and devoted to the service of G-d.

The last day of Sukkot is considered a separate holiday called Shemini Atzeret. It is an extra day (two in the Diaspora) when the Jewish people can enjoy the closeness to G-d that has developed over the High Holidays before returning to daily life. In the words of the verse, "It is a time of retreat" (ibid. 36).

# SIMCHAT TORAH

Simchat Torah, literally the "rejoicing with the Torah," celebrated on the second day of Shemini Atzeret in the Diaspora (in Israel on the first), is the culmination of the High Holidays. On Simchat Torah, we read the final portion in the Torah scroll and immediately begin anew from the beginning of Genesis.

The central focus of the day, however, is dancing. The Torah scrolls are removed from the ark and carried around the reading table in the synagogue seven times, still wrapped in their coverings. Verses are recited each time the crowd circles the table, and then joyous dancing commences.

While scholarly study may not be accessible to all, the greatest Torah scholar and the unlearned person are on equal footing on Simchat Torah, emphasizing that the Torah belongs to all.

# HANUKKAH

*Hanukkah is the eight-day holiday marking the rededication of the second Holy Temple after it was defiled by the Syrian Greeks in the year 139 BCE.*

In 151 BCE, the Syrian Greeks and the Hellenists, a group of assimilated Jews, began a scheme to eliminate Jewish practice in the Land of Israel. Anyone caught observing the Sabbath or performing circumcisions and traditional Jewish weddings was punished.

After close to a decade of religious persecution, Matityahu and his children, members of the priestly family, led a revolt, beginning in the city of Modiin in central Israel, against the much larger Greek army. The ensuing war lasted for close to two years, but the small army of Jews was ultimately victorious, "Where G-d placed the mighty in the hands of the weak, and the many in the hands of the few," and regained control of their homeland.

Their first order of business was to repair and restore the Holy Temple in Jerusalem, which the Greeks had desecrated. Searching among the ruins for olive oil to kindle the Temple's golden candelabra, they miraculously discovered only one flask that had not been contaminated. It should have lasted for only one day, but the oil famously burned for eight, enough time for the Jews to produce more. We commemorate this miracle by kindling one additional light on a candelabra (*menorah*) on each night of Hanukkah, culminating on the eighth night when eight candles are lit.

The menorah is lit in the evening, so that the lights will be noticeable. Some place the menorah on the windowsill, as long as it is less than twenty-nine feet above the ground, or by the door, to fulfill the directive of the sages to "publicize the miracle." Potato latkes and doughnuts, both fried in oil, are traditional Hanukkah fare, and the *sevivon*, or *dreidel*, a four sided top that children used to conceal illicit Torah study from the Greeks, is the children's game of choice.

The lessons of the menorah are simple and powerful: We should always be adding light—good deeds—to the world. Yesterday's effort is not enough for today. And a little bit of light can dispel much darkness.

# TU B'SHEVAT

## NEW YEAR FOR TREES

*The fifteenth of the Jewish month of Shevat (January or February) is the New Year for trees in the Land of Israel, when the sap begins to rise and a new growing season begins.*

Tu B'Shevat is especially significant in Israel, where everyone is obligated to separate part of their produce each year for various tithes (in the times of the Temple, it was donated to various causes, such as the priests or Levites).

It is thus a day to celebrate and enjoy the fruits and grains traditionally associated with the Land of Israel: dates, pomegranates, barley, wheat, grapes, figs, and olives. These require a special blessing to be recited afterward, thanks to a famous passage in Deuteronomy: "For the L-rd, your G-d, is bringing you to a good land, a land with brooks of water, fountains, and depths that emerge in valleys and mountains, a land of wheat and barley, vines and figs, and pomegranates, a land of oil-producing olives and honey.... And you will eat and be sated, and you shall bless the L-rd, your G-d, for the good land He has given you" (8:7–10).

In order to be able to recite the blessing for special occasions, many also partake of a fruit that they did not taste yet in the season: "Blessed are You, L-rd our G-d, King of the universe, who has granted us life, sustained us, and enabled us to reach this occasion."

The deeper significance of Tu B'Shevat can be found in another verse in Deuteronomy: "For man is a tree of the field" (20:19). Among the many parallels between people and trees: children, our saplings, need to be nourished and supported in order to grow properly; good deeds, our fruit, should contain seeds that will reproduce, inspiring others to follow our example; and, like our leafy analogues, we need strong roots (faith) to survive the storms of life.

# PURIM

*The fourteenth day of the Jewish month of Adar (February or March) is Purim, a holiday that celebrates the Jews' miraculous escape from extermination in the year 356 BCE.*

The story of Purim, recounted in the Book of Esther, is one of political intrigue rather than explicit miracles. In the year 366 BCE, Ahasuerus took control of the Persian Empire. Soon afterward, he made a large banquet, during which, in a drunken rage, he ordered his wife to be executed. Having made a survey of all the young women in his kingdom, he selected a Jewish girl who took the name Esther, meaning "hidden" (she did not reveal her nationality), to replace her. Esther's cousin, Mordechai, was the leader of the Jewish people in that generation.

Five years later, the king fell under the influence of his advisor Haman, who, enraged by Mordechai's refusal to bow before him, concocted a scheme to annihilate the Jews. At Mordechai's urging, Esther approached the king and begged for mercy, "For we have been sold, I and my people, to be destroyed, to be slain, and to perish" (Esther 7:4). The king had Haman and his sons hanged and gave Mordechai his job.

Purim means "lotteries," because Haman selected the day on which the Jews were to be killed (the 13th of Adar) by drawing lots. Thanks to Esther's intervention, the Jews successfully defended themselves and celebrated the following day as a holiday (the actual day, marked at the time by Esther as a day of prayer and fasting, is still observed as a fast day).

Today, Purim is celebrated by reading the Book of Esther, eating a festive meal, sending gifts of food to friends, and giving charity to the poor. It is also customary to dress in costume, a nod to the role deception played in the story. Not only did Esther conceal her identity from the king, but G-d concealed His role in the story, making it appear to be merely the result of fortuitous events. This is also the significance of *hamentashen*, triangular cookies that conceal their fruit filling, traditionally eaten on Purim.

The everyday nature of the Purim miracle is a reminder of the innumerable miracles that make up our daily lives. Just as the Jews looked behind the mask of chance, represented by the lottery, and celebrated their victory as a gift from G-d, so too one should look beyond "coincidence" and acknowledge the divine providence that permeates every moment of their life.

# PASSOVER

*Passover, the eight-day holiday celebrating the Israelites' Exodus from Egypt, begins on the fifteenth of the Hebrew month of Nissan (March or April).*

The book of Exodus describes how, in 1429 BCE, just over a century after Jacob and his family moved to Egypt, a new Pharaoh came to power and, fearing that in case of war the Jews would form a fifth column, forced them into slavery for over one hundred years. Despite a decree that all Israelite baby boys be thrown into the Nile, many were saved, including Moses, who ultimately led his people to freedom in the year 1313 BCE.

The holiday gets its name from a lesser-known episode in the story: Before the last of the ten plagues, G-d told the Israelites to slaughter sheep (not incidentally, the Egyptians worshipped sheep) and smear the blood on the doorposts of their homes. Then, when the angel of death came to take the firstborn sons of the Egyptians, it *passed over* the homes of the Jews, which were thus marked. During Temple times, the Pascal sacrifice was offered on the altar each year in Jerusalem.

The story, including the Splitting of the Sea of Reeds (known as the Red Sea) and the drowning of the Egyptian army, is recounted at the Seder, a ritual meal on the first and second (in the Diaspora) nights of the holiday. The centerpiece of the Seder is matzah, cracker-like bread that commemorates the loaves the Israelites took on their journey—they left in such a hurry that they did not have time to let their bread rise.

During the entire eight days (seven in Israel), leavened foods (e.g., bread or cookies) are not permitted in one's house, as the verse states (Exodus 12:15), "Eat matzah for seven days. On the eve of this day, you must have your homes cleared of all leaven." Much of the preparation for the holiday involves cleaning away leavened food items that may be anywhere in the home.

The Seder is a reenactment of the Exodus: We eat bitter herbs to remember the bitterness of slavery; a vegetable dipped into saltwater recalls the tears of the Israelites. A mixture of fruit and ground nuts resembles the cement the slaves used to build the Egyptian cities, and an egg and shank bone remind us of the pascal and the general holiday sacrifices.

Four cups of wine, spread out over the course of the Seder, correspond to four expressions of redemption (ibid. 6:6–7), "I am G-d, I will take you away from your forced labor ... free you ... liberate you ... and will take you to Myself as a nation," and recall the four Jewish matriarchs: Sarah, Rebecca, Rachel, and Leah.

The main purpose of the Seder, however, is to transmit the story of the Exodus to the next generation. "You shall tell your child on that day," (Exodus 13:4). In perhaps the most famous passage of the *Hagaddah*, the text recited at the Seder, the children ask their parents, "Why is this night different from all other nights?" The remainder of the book is dedicated to the answer and to thanking G-d for our salvation. Innumerable scholarly works have been devoted to expounding the *Hagaddah*. Indeed, it is one of the most studied pieces of Jewish liturgy.

The Hebrew word for Egypt shares a root with the word meaning "boundaries" or "limitations." The Exodus, then, is an ongoing process. Each year, we experience it on a deeper level, freeing ourselves from our inner slave-masters: insecurity, doubt, fear, bad habits, and our negative inclinations.

The unleavened bread represents humility. Passover is an opportunity to reflect on our shortcomings and the ways in which we could use our gifts to better serve humanity and our Creator.

# LAG B'OMER

Forty-nine days separate Passover from the festival of Shavuot, the anniversary of the Giving of the Torah. These seven weeks are a time of introspection and self-refinement—the Torah commands us to bring the *omer* offering of barley in the Temple on the second day of Passover, representing the elevation of the animalistic tendencies to G-d (barley was considered animal fodder), and to count each day individually from then onward.

Later, these days also became a time of mourning, as it was during this period that most of the twenty-four thousand students of the first-century sage Rabbi Akiva died, because, our sages tell us, they did not treat each other with sufficient respect. On the thirty-third day, however, the plague abated.

The day is also the anniversary of the passing of Rabbi Shimon bar Yochai, who figures prominently in the Mishnah and is known for his Kabbalistic teachings. Before his death, Rabbi Shimon requested that the day be celebrated as a holiday, and until today, the most joyous celebrations of the thirty-third (pronounced "lag" in Hebrew) day of the Omer take place at his gravesite in Meron, Israel. Outside of the Holy Land, Lag B'Omer is celebrated with picnics, bonfires, and events to promote love and unity among Jewish people.

# SHAVUOT

On the sixth of the Hebrew month of Sivan, around seven weeks after leaving Egypt, the Israelites received the Torah (see *Torah*) on Mount Sinai. Shavuot, the anniversary of this pivotal event, is a two-day holiday in the Diaspora, celebrated in the early summer (May or June). Shavuot literally means "weeks," a reference to the seven-week Omer period (see *Lag B'Omer*) that precedes it.

The Torah itself gives a detailed account of the event: the young nation, estimated at two million, gathered at the foot of the desert mountain for a direct revelation from G-d: "There were thunder claps and lightning flashes, and a thick cloud was upon the mountain, and a very powerful blast of a ram's horn, and the entire nation that was in the camp shuddered ... [and] G-d spoke all these words" (Exodus 19:16).

In fact, the sages tell us that G-d spoke only the first two of the Ten Commandments, "I am G-d, who took you out of the land of Egypt," and "You shall have no other gods before me," directly to the people. The experience was so intense that the Israelites begged Moses to serve as an intermediary, which he did, ascending the mountain and relaying the remaining eight commandments. He then remained on the mountain for an additional forty-day conversation with the Almighty, returning with the famous tablets.

Never before, nor afterward, in the history of the world did such a large number of people claim to have direct contact with the divine. While Jews notoriously disagree on many aspects of Jewish life, the fact that this story has been told over and over, by the descendants of those who were present, until our times, is powerful evidence of its truth.

The main event of Shavuot is the reading of the Ten Commandments. Even those who do not normally attend synagogue, especially young children, are encouraged to be present. It is also customary to spend the first night of the holiday studying rather than sleeping as atonement for our ancestors, who, the sages tell us, slept in on the morning the Torah was given.

Several other customs associated with the holiday: We eat a dairy meal on the first day, because the first Shavuot was on the Sabbath, and the nation could not put into practice their newly received commandments regarding kosher meat (see *Kosher*). To bring the holiday joy, synagogues and homes are decorated with greenery and flowers, which also remind us of the greenery on Mount Sinai. And many read the Book of Ruth, because she was a convert to Judaism and, like the Israelites at Mount Sinai, voluntarily accepted all the obligations of the Torah.

Shavuot is called the time of the *Giving of the Torah*, not, the sages point out, of our receiving it. Receiving the Torah, accepting it as divine wisdom and incorporating it into our lives, is a life-long endeavor.

# TISHA B'AV

The ninth day of the Hebrew month of Av culminates three weeks of mourning over the destruction of the Holy Temples in Jerusalem. It is the saddest day on the Jewish calendar.

The Holy Temple in Jerusalem, built on the Temple Mount, was the place where G-d's presence was openly visible, and Jews would make the pilgrimage from all over the Holy Land three times a year to offer sacrifices from their personal livestock.

In the summer of 423 BCE, the army of Nebuchadnezzar II, the king of Babylon, captured Jerusalem. On the 17th of the Jewish month of Tammuz, the service in the Holy Temple ceased, and three weeks later, on the 9th of Av, the Temple was set ablaze. The Jews were exiled to

Babylon, their precious observance crippled—from the 613 biblical commandments, 244 became inapplicable.

In 349 BCE, the second Holy Temple was completed, and the mourning ceased. However, after close to 420 years, circa 69 CE, the Temple was destroyed once again, this time by the Romans, and over a million Jews died in war and from famine and sickness. According to tradition, both Temples were destroyed on the 9th day of Av.

Tisha B'Av is a fast day (one of several marking stages in the Temples' destruction. Others are the 3rd of Tishrei, the 10th of Tevet, and the 17th of Tammuz). We read the book of Lamentations, and observe the stringent rules applicable to mourners, including sitting on low chairs until midday. The day is not devoid of hope, however. It is said that the Messiah was born on this day, a sign that from destruction, there will always arise redemption.

## NOTE TO THE READER

As its title implies, this book is merely a summary. It is in no way intended as a definitive explanation of Jewish thought or observance, and many details, differences of opinion, and customs have been omitted for the sake of brevity.

The explanations of the commandments rely heavily on the thirteenth-century *Sefer HaChinuch (Book of Education)* and on Hasidic philosophy, particularly the teachings of Chabad. Again, these ideas were chosen to give a taste of Jewish thought and are not intended to exclude the multitude of interpretations and philosophies that make Jewish study such a rich and rewarding experience.

While there are various opinions about when many of the events mentioned here transpired, we have chosen to follow *Codex Judaica: Chronological Index of Jewish History*, by Rabbi Mattis Kantor.

Statements attributed to "the sages" are primarily from the Talmud, though occasionally they may come from the Midrash or later rabbinical sources. For ease of reading, we have included sources only for direct quotes from the Pentateuch. Most of these are from the translations of Aryeh Kaplan in *The Living Torah* and *The Living Nach*, courtesy of Moznaim Publishing and its director, Menachem Vagshal.

It is our hope that the work will serve as a springboard to further study.

# Acknowledgements

I dedicate this book to my grandfather Rabbi Chaim Meir Bukiet, who led his community in East Flatbush, Brooklyn, until his passing twenty years ago. Several of the books I inherited from his library were used in my research.

The idea for this book was originally suggested by Rabbi Menachem Katz of the Aleph Institute. It is in part thanks to his dedication that this book was made possible.

My thanks to those who contributed their ideas, critique, and corrections: Rabbis Nochem Kaplan, Sholom Ber Schuchat, Sholom Zirkind, and Peretz Mochkin. Sarah Ogince fine-tuned the text, making it user-friendly and enjoyable, and Mimi Palace did the final copyedit. My thanks to Mushka Kanner for the design and layout.

I am sincerely grateful to Sholom and Kayla Kramer, whose kindness has made this and many of our other projects possible.

Finally, I thank my wife, Chana Raizel, and my children, Motti, Meir, Shaina, Benny, and Mendel, for their assistance and patience while I was working on this project.

*Dovid*

# Index

MORE FROM DOVID ZAKLIKOWSKI

**Dear Rebbe**
*Rabbi Menachem Mendel Schneerson corresponds with a singer,*
*a writer, a sculptor & a Holocaust survivor*

**Footprints**
*Colorful Lives, Huge Impact*

**Kosher Investigator**
*How Rabbi Berel Levy Built the OK and*
*Transformed the World of Kosher Supervision*